Assessment in Context
A Systems Approach to Educational Effectiveness

Ronald L. Baker

League for Innovation in the Community College

The League for Innovation in the Community College is an international organization dedicated to catalyzing the community college movement. The League hosts conferences and institutes, develops web resources, conducts research, produces publications, provides services, and leads projects and initiatives with more than 750 member colleges, 100 corporate partners, and a host of other government and nonprofit agencies in a continuing effort to make a positive difference for students and communities. Information about the League and its activities is available at www.league.org.

The opinions expressed in this book are those of the author and do not necessarily reflect the views of the League for Innovation in the Community College.

Requests for permission should be sent to
League for Innovation in the Community College
4505 E. Chandler Boulevard, Suite 250
Phoenix, AZ 85048
Email: publications@league.org
Fax: (480) 705-8201

Copies of this monograph are available through the League website at www.league.org, or by calling (480) 705-8200. The publication is also available in digital form through iStream at www.league.org/istream.

Please cite this publication as follows:
Baker, R. L. (2005). *Assessment in Context: A Systems Approach to Educational Effectiveness*. Phoenix: League for Innovation in the Community College.

Printed in the United States of America

ISBN 1-931300-438

Prologue

The purpose of this monograph is to provoke thought and promote dialogue on effective educational practice. Based on the premise that community college practice is a system of interdependent events, it asserts that alignment of those events positively affects fulfillment of personal and institutional intentions. Alignment can be enhanced by analyzing component events within the system and synthesizing relationships among those events. While analysis of individual events in isolation increases knowledge of their functions, it offers little insight into relationships among them. Synthesizing relationships among events, however, fosters understanding of patterns of practice to better align actions and assessments with intentions.

Context is an essential tool for analysis and syntheses. It is important for two reasons. Context helps in gaining insight into expectations that influence higher education's function and purpose. It also aids in selecting assessment strategies, methods, and tools to determine if intentions are fulfilled at acceptable levels of quality and effectiveness. As a first step to understanding the context for perspectives expressed in this monograph, Table 1 provides operational definitions of key terms.

Table 1. Glossary

OPERATIONAL DEFINITIONS

Analysis	Systematic critical examination of data to acquire knowledge of properties
Assessment	Purposeful process of analysis and synthesis to authenticate, appraise, and document achievements, quality, and effectiveness
Assimilation	Use of evidence-based conclusions to inform and improve practice
Collection	Systematic acquisition of data linked to indicators of outcomes achievement
Context	Interrelated conditions and influences that shroud, shape, and explain an event
Evaluation	Meaning derived from analysis
Evidence	Documentation to support judgments, conclusions, and actions
Goals	Indicators of achievement in fulfilling mission and vision
Integrity	Agreement of values and intentions with actions and achievements
Intentions	Mission-based aspirations to be fulfilled through focused planning and action
Mission	Translation of values and intentions into purpose
Outcome	Result achieved through a structured sequence of actions
Principles	Basic beliefs accepted as true
Synthesis	Integration of analyses to achieve understanding of relationships and purpose
System	Set of elements that interact to form a whole in such a way that compromising a relationship among elements compromises the purpose of the whole
Values	Meritorious principles or qualities that guide action and behavior
Vision	Institutional target for complete fulfillment of its purpose

A Systems Approach to Educational Effectiveness

A fundamental tenet of systems theory is that understanding a system is enhanced by identifying and analyzing its elements, complemented by a synthesis of the elements' roles and interactions within the system (Ackoff, 1995). Analysis takes the system apart by focusing on its individual elements in isolation to gain knowledge of their properties, structures, and functions. Synthesis puts the system together in a holistic manner by focusing on the roles and relationships among the elements to gain understanding of the system's purpose and meaning. Based on the assumption that community college practice is a system of interrelated elements that requires both analysis of elements and synthesis of relationships among those elements, systems theory is chosen as the philosophical foundation for this monograph.

After years of effort, higher education continues to struggle with assessment (Angelo, 2002). The academy's efforts, however, have not been fruitless. The literature contains considerable information on various elements of practice (Banta, 2002). Over the past few decades, much has been written on assessment, and an impressive inventory of assessment tools has been developed (Assessment Framework, 2004). While the means of assessment are clearly important and generally understood, misalignment of a tool with the purpose of the assessment frequently generates more frustration than fulfillment by producing results that have little, if any, meaning (Pike, 2002). The effectiveness and value of assessment can be enhanced by balancing an existing knowledge and skill in *how* to assess with a clearer understanding of the *context* for the conduct of assessment.

Context for Assessment

Community colleges have traditionally reflected society's values and needs (O'Banion, 1997). Those values and needs, however, are undergoing a dramatic shift (Baker, 2001). Narrow focus and polarizing partisanship replace comprehensive vision and unifying compromise; self-indulgence and immediate gratification displace sacrifice and sustaining investment; personal prerogative overshadows social responsibility; individual agendas supersede reasoned judgments; monologue is mistaken for dialogue; sound bites substitute for debate;

tolerance is spoken, but intolerance is practiced; complexity of solutions is inversely proportional to the complexity of the problems being solved; the ethics of personal and professional conduct are determined by the risk of exposure; common sense is a quaint antiquated notion that is presumed, but seldom exhibited; and a sense of entitlement permeates society with an assignment of culpability seemingly more important than assuming personal responsibility for individual actions driven more by what can be done than what should be done.

The shift of societal values and needs is producing a corresponding shift in policies that influence educational practice. Considerations of capacity and efficiency replace concerns for access and opportunity, responsiveness to accountability requirements replaces attention to continuous improvement, and conformity and external control replace institutional diversity and autonomy. Foremost among the consequences of the shift is a fundamental reconsideration of the meaning of educational quality and effectiveness that leads inevitably to a reassessment of the purpose and function of higher education (Gardiner, 1994).

Throughout most of their history, community colleges were viewed as a social advocacy archetype to meet the needs of society by developing human capital. They stimulated personal and societal advancement by developing individual human potential that, when aggregated, benefited society as a whole. As a result, socioeconomic mobility and personal, societal, and economic vitality were strengthened through an expansion of access to a broad range of educational programs. Judgments of educational quality and effectiveness were commonly based on inferred outcomes, perceptions of performance, and implications of achievements rather than explicit evidence of accomplishments (Peters, 1994). Descriptions of intentions, strength of infrastructure, and magnitude of assets were generally sufficient to demonstrate fulfillment of institutional intentions.

Currently, however, community colleges are regarded as an economic accountability archetype to meet business needs in gaining competitive commercial advantage (Gardiner, 1994). Educational effectiveness is evaluated not in terms of personal or societal growth and development, but in terms of positive returns on investments of fiscal, physical, and human resources (Ewell, 1994). Direct outcomes that are easily evaluated by economic metrics are more easily understood and supported than indirect qualitative humanistic outcomes. Nonetheless, in the current climate of accountability, all outcomes, whether short term or long term, social based or economic based, ineffable or definable, are expected to be explicitly identified, assessed, achieved, and documented rather than merely assumed or implied (Wolff & Harris, 1994). One consequence of this shift of educational archetypes is that some colleagues feel suspended between the idealism of deeply held social values and the realism of economic accountability (Palmer, cited in Gardiner, 1994). They fear that an undue and perhaps unwarranted emphasis on assessment will produce an inevitable decline of mission diversity and instructional innovation, leading to an increase in educational utilitarianism and conformity (Ewell, 2002).

While the academic community has long been the primary adjudicator of educational quality and effectiveness, that role has diminished in recent years. That decline of autonomy is due in part to a decrease in public confidence in the academy's ability to deliver on its promises (Baker, 2001). Specifically, there is growing doubt regarding the efficacy, relevance, and significance of traditional academic credentials such as grades, certificates, and degrees as meaningful indicators of institutional and student achievements (Wilson, Miles, Baker, & Schoenberger, 2000). Absent a proactive response to these doubts, higher education has been perceived by some stakeholders as lacking the will, ability, or capacity to provide evidence-based documentation that institutional intentions are effectively fulfilled (Munitz, 1995). Not surprisingly, then, traditional assessment criteria are being replaced with economic-based criteria such as tuition costs, graduation rates, and time to completion as the basis for independent external judgments of educational quality and effectiveness (Kelly, 1993). Clearly, the purpose of these criteria is to gauge production efficiency and justify expenditures. However, in light of the complexity and scope of community college missions, these efficiency-based criteria may be overly simplistic, unrealistic, and only marginally informative in evaluating the true value and direct contribution of community colleges to personal, societal, and economic vitality.

Since indicators of success such as employment statistics are immediately available and quantifiable, data-driven evidence of quality and effectiveness is relatively straightforward for job entry and career development components of college missions. Evidence of achievement of more general overarching components of institutional missions is more difficult to produce. Achievement of outcomes such as lifelong learning, diversity and acceptance of differences, and self-actualization is frequently long term, indirect, and difficult to quantify. Nonetheless, community colleges are expected to provide evidence of effectiveness in fulfilling their comprehensive missions, including achievement of long-term abstract outcomes as well as short-term concrete outcomes.

Community colleges deserve partial credit and bear partial responsibility for the current emphasis on assessment and evidence of achievements. Developing critical thinkers has long been one of the fundamental cornerstones of community college missions (Gardiner, 1994). Students are not only expected to understand the concept of critical thinking, they are expected to apply it. As a result of the academy's success in producing a population of critical thinkers, college stakeholders expect colleges to validate their claims, fulfill their intentions, and achieve their intended outcomes. While continuing to be informed by institutional judgments, they increasingly rely on their own independently drawn conclusions regarding educational quality and institutional effectiveness.

Subscription to assessment in and of itself, however, does not signal abandonment of traditional educational values. Social-based values can be maintained while simultaneously responding to increased expectations for evidence of achievements. Assessment, properly interpreted and applied in context, is a meaningful and powerful vehicle to evaluate, document, and assure educational quality and effectiveness; foster quality improvement; provide a regular systematic feedback mechanism for students, staff, faculty, and administrators regarding growth and performance; and aid in assessing personal and professional fulfillment.

Assessment in Context

Although educational quality and effectiveness are two of the most deeply held community college values, there is little evidence of agreement on characteristics of quality, indicators of achievement, and criteria for assessment (Baker, 2004). Given the different and passionately held viewpoints of those within the college community, a lack of common understanding is not surprising. If not for increasing pressure from external constituencies, there might be little motivation to move beyond individualized interpretations of quality and effectiveness (Gray, 2002).

The historical perspective is that quality and effectiveness are directly related to the quality of institutional intentions and capacity. Consequently, judgments were based on assessments of institutional inputs, most notably infrastructures, processes, resources, and teaching practices (Baker, 2004). However, judgments based solely on assessments of resources and processes are no longer acceptable (Boggs, 1995). Increasingly, the perspective of external stakeholders is that quality and effectiveness are directly related to institutional efficiency and economy with an evaluation of effectiveness based on throughput, achievement of results, and return on investments. These two worldviews can be bridged with assessment as the connector, if assessment is conducted in the proper context for the right reasons.

For purposes of this monograph, assessment is defined as a purposeful process of analysis and synthesis to authenticate, appraise, explain, and document achievements. It is an overarching term for a system consisting of five major components: (1) collection, (2) analysis, (3) evaluation, (4) evidence, and (5) assimilation. Conducting meaningful assessment is the product of a conscious alignment of these five components. Collectively, they help ensure congruence of principles, values, intentions, actions, and achievements by aligning institutional infrastructures, resources, and processes. A precursor to that alignment is a clear understanding of institutional principles and values and their influence on practice.

A community college's values, such as open access to a comprehensive array of educational opportunities, academic quality, and teaching effectiveness, are the heart of the institution, its reason for existence and guide for all it does (Carver, 1997). Its values are reflected in its mission and manifested through actions that lead to fulfillment of intentions. Institutional integrity is maintained by continuous assessment of achievements to ensure principles and values are preserved and intentions are fulfilled at acceptable levels of quality and effectiveness. Individually and in relation with each other, values, mission, action, and evaluation inform and guide practice. (See Figure 1.)

Figure 1. Pyramid of Guided Practice

QUESTIONS FOR REFLECTION: PRINCIPLES, VALUES, MISSION, AND VISION
1. Is your institution on a mission or does it simply have a mission?
2. What are your institution's principles and values?
3. Are they reflected in its mission and vision?
4. Do values and mission guide planning and decision making?
5. How are they manifested in daily practice?

Intentions

Institutional intentions, most notably student learning outcomes, are the cornerstones of community college missions. However, expectations and outcomes are typically stated in broad general terms rather than statements of specific knowledge, skills, abilities, and attitudes completing students are expected to demonstrate (Gardiner, 1994). Without clarity on the intended outcomes, it is difficult to know what to assess or how to assess achievements. Other than program requirements, institutions provide little information on how program-level and institutional-level outcomes are acquired and how they relate to course-level outcomes.

Relationships between levels of outcomes do exist, but are more commonly inferred than articulated. Observations of educational practice might suggest that institutions operate on general assumptions that (1) successful completion of courses is evidence of student achievement of intended course outcomes, (2) successful completion of a specified program of study equates to achievement of intended program-level learning outcomes, and (3) successful completion of institutional requirements means intended institutional-level learning outcomes have been achieved. Are these assumptions valid? Do they provide sufficient evidence to warrant public confidence that intended outcomes are achieved?

Institutional learning outcomes are broad and cross-discipline in nature. Examples include effective communication, an ability to work independently and in teams, and an ability to think critically and solve problems. Given their overarching and frequently summative interrelated nature, it is unlikely that institutional-level learning outcomes are achieved in an individual course, department, program, or co-curricular activity. It is reasonable, however, to conclude they are achieved through an accumulation and synthesis of outcomes of multiple courses or co-curricular activities.

Program-level outcomes are designed to foster success in the field associated with the program of study. They may also contribute directly or indirectly, substantially or incidentally to achievement of overarching institutional-level outcomes. Program-level outcomes are achieved by aggregating and leveraging course-level outcomes. Course-level outcomes are narrowly focused and discipline specific in nature. Although they are aligned primarily with program-level outcomes, they can contribute to achievement of one or more institutional-level outcomes. The following example illustrates an articulation between course-level, program-level, and institutional-level outcomes to foster confidence in the institution's ability to fulfill its intentions.

Example 1. Relating Levels of Outcomes. Assume that functioning effectively in a changing world is an institutional-level outcome, Business Administration is a program of study, and World Cultures is a required course for the Business Administration program. Assume further that one of the outcomes for the Business Administration program is an ability to conduct business in a global economy and that one of the outcomes for the World Cultures course is development of an understanding of human values and their influence on perspectives and actions. One can reasonably argue that developing a global perspective of human values contributes to an ability to effectively conduct business in a global environment and simultaneously fosters the creation of a social awareness that promotes meaningful and successful interaction in a world of diverse values, perspectives, and contexts. The point of this example is that relationships between levels of outcomes can be articulated. Identifying and stating these relationships serves two primary purposes: (1) It forces the academy to review what it does, why it does it, and how the pieces fit together; and (2) it provides institutions with a clear map of pathways and milestones to assure students and the public at large of the credibility and relevance of their educational programs.

QUESTIONS FOR REFLECTION: INTENTIONS
1. Are intended outcomes and expectations identified?
2. Are they explicitly stated or implicitly inferred?
3. Are they congruent with institutional values and mission?
4. Are they identified at institutional, program or unit, and course or activity levels?
5. What are the indicators of success in meeting expectations and achieving intended outcomes?

Actions

Some within the academic community may argue that traditional delivery and assessment practices are adequate to address the interests and concerns of external stakeholders. They claim setting program and degree requirements, developing and delivering courses, conducting student examinations, and assigning grades are sufficient to demonstrate the rigor, relevance, and quality of student learning. Many outside the academic community, however, disagree and cite a need for more meaningful and explicit evidence of achievements (Wolff & Harris, 1994). Articulating relationships between intentions, actions, and accomplishments is one way to identify needed changes to practice as well as to enhance confidence in the academy's ability to deliver on its promises. Consider the following example.

Example 2. Misaligned Actions. The intended outcome for a Writing 101 class is defined as follows: Students will write an effective college-level position paper exhibiting focus, organization, style, content, structure, logic, and mechanics at generally recognized and accepted levels of quality and effectiveness. Active learning is stated as the theoretical foundation for achieving the course outcome, and lecture is the method of instruction. Student learning activities consist of readings from a list of reserved materials in the library, augmented by peer group discussions. (See Figure 2.) It must be noted that there is nothing inherently wrong with any of these actions. For some courses with different outcomes, they might be very effective in fostering achievement of the intended outcome. Yet for this course, they appear to be actions of convenience. While they may enhance a student's awareness and knowledge of writing, they do little to develop actual student writing abilities.

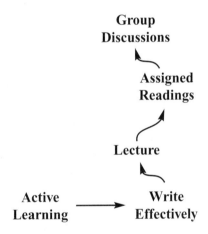

Figure 2. Principles, Intentions, and Actions

There are, of course, many factors that influence decisions regarding teaching and learning activities. A clear understanding of the intended outcomes and actions for achieving those outcomes is essential in guiding selection and implementation of appropriate actions and assessment strategies. Consider the following examples.

Example 3. Alignment of Actions: Surface Learning. A Medical Terminology class is required for a Medical Receptionist associate degree program. One of the intended outcomes for the class is correct spelling, definition, usage, and pronunciation of medical terms based on an ability to recognize, spell, and use prefixes, suffixes, word roots, special endings, plural forms, abbreviations, and symbols Because these outcomes are fairly straightforward and easy to demonstrate and assess, objective, clear, and widely accepted evaluation criteria can be used.

Example 4. Alignment of Actions: Deep Learning. An Anatomy and Physiology class is required for an Associate Degree in Nursing program. There are two outcomes for this class. One outcome, like the outcome for the Medical Terminology class, is knowledge and correct use of vocabulary associated with human anatomy. The second outcome requires description and understanding of the basic structure and function of each major human biological system. Achievement of the first outcome is fairly straightforward to effect and evaluate. Understanding of structures and functions is more abstract, so evaluation criteria are typically more subjective, less commonly defined, and subject to individual interpretation.

Examples 3 and 4 identify an outcome relating to knowledge and correct use of medical terminology. Achieving that outcome requires an accumulation, recognition, and mastery of concrete factual information. Use of lecture, flash cards, and spelling quizzes might be appropriate to effect that intended outcome. Understanding structures and functions requires a deeper level of study, analysis, and synthesis to identify the component parts of the biological systems and, more importantly, explain how the parts function individually and collectively. To achieve understanding, laboratory observations and experiments, simulations, and discussions are more appropriate methods of instruction. In each example, identification and understanding of the intended course outcomes and the learning theory associated with their achievement guide the selection of effective teaching and learning actions to support student success.

QUESTIONS FOR REFLECTION: ACTIONS

1. What steps are taken to fulfill institutional mission and goals?
2. What steps are taken to realize purposes and achieve intended outcomes for institutional units?
3. What steps are taken to achieve intended educational program outcomes?
4. What steps are taken to facilitate student achievement of intended educational outcomes?
5. Do these actions align with institutional principles, values, and purpose?

Assessment

One of the main purposes of assessment is to evaluate and document achievements. An important consideration in fulfilling that purpose is the level of analysis required. For example, assessment to evaluate student learning achievements is quite different from assessment to evaluate institutional effectiveness. Assessment of institutional and program effectiveness typically employs criteria such as course completion, student persistence, and graduation rates to measure institutional efficiency in effecting student completion of degrees and certificates within specific periods of time. These criteria, however, may not reflect institutional success in meeting student, employer, or societal needs, because they assume students are well prepared for college-level study, clear on their choice of program, and have the luxury of enrolling on a continuous full-time basis. They further assume that students who do not finish a complete program of study are ill prepared to meet employer needs. These assumptions are false, since the vast majority of community and technical college students do not possess characteristics of readiness, focus, and flexibility of time (CCSSE, 2004). Consequently, judgments of institutional effectiveness based on rates of retention and graduation or time to completion may have little correlation to the actual effectiveness of an institution or program in meeting society's educational needs.

Assessing individual student success is much more complex than assessing institutional and program effectiveness, because student objectives and indicators of success are as varied as the students themselves. Therefore, aggregating assessments of individual student success may yield little useful information in judging institutional and program effectiveness. For example, a student may enroll at an institution to upgrade work skills by taking a cluster of classes that constitutes part, but not all, of an associate degree program. Work, financial, or personal commitments might limit the student's enrollment to alternating terms. Upon successfully completing the desired cluster of courses over several years of part-time attendance, the student terminates enrollment. Although the student's and the employer's expectations are met, persistence and completion statistics indicate the institution and program were not effective, because the student did not complete the entire program of study within a traditionally defined two-year period of time.

The context for assessment is, therefore, essential to guide the selection of meaningful and informative criteria, methods, and data. Quality and effectiveness can be assessed in a number of areas, including (1) student learning, (2) teaching effectiveness, (3) educational program effectiveness, (4) institutional unit effectiveness, (5) overall institutional effectiveness, and (6) personal fulfillment. Nuances associated with each of these intentions are sufficient to influence actions and interpretations of findings.

Student learning focuses on achievement of intended learning outcomes. Assessment of student learning is designed for evaluation of authentic student achievements of identified learning outcomes. Teaching effectiveness concentrates on teaching strategies and practices. Assessment of teaching effectiveness evaluates student engagement in the learning process. Educational program effectiveness is based on subject area and external stakeholder expectations. Program assessment evaluates student success in the field. Institutional unit-level effectiveness is based on organizational responsibilities. Unit-level assessment evaluates the unit's success in fulfilling its role and purpose. Institutional effectiveness focuses on inputs, processes, and achievements. Integrity is evaluated by assessment of fulfillment of institutional intentions. Personal fulfillment concentrates on personal expectations, effectiveness, and satisfaction. Personal assessment evaluates an individual's peace of mind, contentment of heart, and tranquility of soul.

Assessment effectiveness depends, at least partially, on the outcome to be assessed. A tool that provides direct evidence of achievement in one situation may provide only indirect evidence, at best, of achievement in another situation. For example, a perception survey may reveal that students think they achieved intended outcomes, but yield little direct evidence of actual achievement of those outcomes. On the other hand, if an intended outcome for student services is providing an environment in which students feel welcome and honored, then a perception survey provides direct and meaningful evidence of student feelings on those topics. Therefore, knowing the intended outcome and assessment rationale provides context for the selection of strategies and tools that enhance the value and usefulness of assessment findings. To reinforce the influence of intentions on assessment, consider another example.

Example 5. Levels of Analysis and Evaluation. Assume the purposes for assessment in a nursing class are to evaluate teaching effectiveness and student achievement. An examination is administered and a student receives a score of 75 points. With just this data, there is very little information to draw a conclusion regarding student achievements. A score of 75 out of 100 possible points would quite likely produce an entirely different conclusion than a score of 75 out of 500 possible points. For the sake of the example, assume that 100 points is the maximum possible for the test. Simple analysis would indicate that a score of 75 points corresponds to 75 percent of the total possible and, thus, falls into the C range. Therefore, one might conclude the student is of average ability.

What if further analysis reveals that of the 75 points scored on the test, all 75 points were earned from the theory portion and 0 points were earned on the venipuncture practicum portion? Moreover, the student missed a three-point question on the theory section that was also missed by every other student in the class. Finally, a review of the examination scores reveals that a majority of students performed very well on the theory section, but poorly on the venipuncture practicum portion.

There are a number of ways these findings can influence practice. The instructor may wish to revisit the question missed by all students to determine the validity of the question. Awareness of the disparity of learning between theory and practicum might generate a review of the curriculum and instructional delivery of the venipuncture practicum portion of the course. These results might also be used to better inform students regarding areas of strength and areas needing improvement. Potentially, it could influence student decisions on personal interests and abilities that guide career choices. In this example, it might suggest the student is well suited for a career in a medical field that does not require patient venipuncture.

Consider once again the misalignment of outcomes and actions illustrated in Example 2. Assume that assessment of students' effective writing abilities, the intended class outcome, consists of a multiple-choice test and survey of student perceptions of their writing abilities. Assume further that class attendance and participation in small group discussions are factored into the final grade, which is determined by a bell-curve distribution of points acquired during the term. (See Figure 3.)

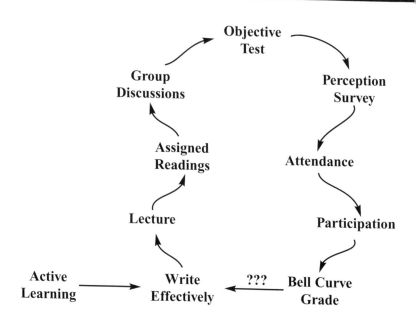

Figure 3. Principles, Intentions, Actions, and Assessment

It is hard to argue that principles, intentions, actions, assessments, analyses, and judgments represented in this example provide evidence that inspires confidence of student achievement of the intended outcome. Once again, there is nothing inherently wrong with any individual course assessment method. While the assessment methods in this example may enable a judgment of a student's knowledge of writing, they are ineffective in providing evidence of the student's writing ability.

This example does not suggest it is typical of institutional practice or that the underlying principles are relevant only for instruction. The point of the example is to present a worst-case scenario for the sole purpose of highlighting the importance of aligning actions and assessments with intended outcomes. Tools and methods should be carefully considered and purposefully selected for their fit and effectiveness, rather than for familiarity or convenience.

Questions for Reflection: Assessment

1. Do outcomes determine what is assessed or does ease of assessment determine outcomes?
2. Are achievements inferred from process completion or affirmed by assessment?
3. Are assessment criteria and methods relevant and meaningful for outcomes being evaluated?
4. How valid and reliable is the assessment of outcomes that cross operational boundaries?
5. Who assesses? Who evaluates results? Are these assessors and evaluators selected for convenience or for effectiveness?

Analysis, Evaluation, and Assimilation

In addition to evaluating achievements, assessment can also be used to sustain areas of effective practice and address areas of ineffective practice. Recall the assessment of student learning outcomes from Example 5. In addition to assessing individual student performance, analysis of test scores disclosed useful information that might generate a review of teaching practices, the curriculum, or assessment methods and tools used to enhance program effectiveness. The following example illustrates the role of assessment in evaluating achievement of program-level outcomes.

Example 6. Program Effectiveness. An applied associate degree program in shoe and leather goods repair is designed to prepare students for success as independent self-employed business owners. A capstone evaluation revealed that all students achieved requisite skills in repairing shoes and leather goods. Six months following graduation, a perception survey was administered, and graduates were found to be well satisfied with the technical content of their program. More than 90 percent of graduates were found to be gainfully employed as sole proprietors in their field of study. However, a follow-up survey conducted three years after graduation revealed that only 40 percent of graduates were still gainfully self-employed in the field. Moreover, the survey revealed that a vast majority of those no longer employed as sole proprietors in the field indicated that while they were well prepared with trade skills, they lacked adequate interpersonal and business skills, such as customer service and bookkeeping, to effectively deal with the public in operating a retail business. These assessment findings are valuable in reviewing the program's curriculum and may result in enhancements to the curriculum to strengthen interpersonal and business skills. Alternatively, they may be useful in making decisions on future directions for the program (*e.g.*, eliminating a program emphasis on self-employment). The point of this example is not what the decision should be, but rather that assessment aids in program evaluation that informs planning and decision making.

Questions for Reflection: Assimilation

1. Does assessment occur on a regular purposeful basis?
2. How are assessment findings used for planning and decision making?
3. How are assessment findings used to improve institutional, unit, and program effectiveness?
4. How are assessment findings used to improve teaching effectiveness and student learning?
5. How are assessment findings used to reinforce personal commitment and enrich satisfaction?

Evidence

Evidence of achievements takes many forms. For student learning, the most common form of evidence is the traditional transcript. However, summary course-level judgments, course descriptors, and grades provide little insight on expected outcomes or specific information on achievement of those outcomes. A better framework for interpreting student learning can be provided in an annotated transcript that lists intended institutional, program, and course descriptions, and program requirements as well as course grades. In addition to providing traditional statements of learning at the course level, annotated transcripts provide context to assist transcript reviewers in drawing meaning from course grades. Even more value can be added by listing intended institutional, program, and course outcomes as well as institutional, program, and course descriptions and grades. Regardless of the form of transcript, student knowledge, skills, abilities, and attitudes can only be inferred due to a lack of evidence of student achievement of intended outcomes.

More direct evidence of student learning is possible within the framework of the transcript construct. In addition to listing courses, grades, descriptions, and intended outcomes at the institutional, program, and course levels, a confirmation of student learning can provide evidence of achievement of those outcomes. Whether simply marked as achieved or not achieved or marked by level of achievement ranging from minimal to mastery, a confirmation of student learning provides richer evidence of student achievements than traditional or annotated transcripts. It also provides more meaningful evidence of accomplishments for interested stakeholders. Even more evidence can be provided in an academic portfolio that includes samples of student work as well as information listed on transcripts or confirmations of student learning.

Questions for Reflection: Evidence

1. What evidence is used to track and document achievements?
2. Is it a summary of overarching achievements or an account of specific achievements?
3. Is it an authentic representation of achievements or a record of processes?
4. How well does it correlate to indicators of success in outcomes achievement?
5. Does it suggest or does it support conclusions regarding quality and effectiveness?

Implications for Practice

If traditional ineffable intentions embedded in community and technical college missions are to persist in the economic accountability archetype, the academy itself must demonstrate that outcomes associated with those intentions can be and are assessed and achieved. While acknowledging that broad overarching outcomes such as lifelong learning, citizenship, and appreciation for and tolerance of differences cannot be fully achieved within the limited timeframe of student enrollment in associate degree programs, contributions toward achievement of those intentions can and must be stated and evaluated. The following example illustrates how achievement of ineffable outcomes can be fostered, achieved, evaluated, and documented.

Example 7. Evaluating the Ineffable. A common community college outcome is student engagement in lifelong learning. Two questions immediately surface regarding this outcome: (1) What is lifelong learning, and (2) what are the indicators of achievement? Achievement of this ineffable outcome is rarely if ever evaluated, since it represents an intention that is presumed to be achieved as a byproduct of completion of a course or program of study. For the purposes of this example, lifelong learning is defined as learning to learn through the acquisition and application of inquiry, critical thinking, and self-directed learning skills to achieve knowledge, understanding, and abilities that enhance the quality and effectiveness of personal, civic, social, and employment success throughout life.

It might be argued that attempting to assess this outcome is difficult, since the majority of lifelong learning takes place outside the institution and beyond the timeframe of student enrollment. That does not mean, however, that some degree of preparation, achievement, and assessment of lifelong learning is not possible. In fact, it is quite possible to evaluate institutional contributions and student progress toward achieving that outcome at the community college level. Embedded in the above definition of lifelong learning is an expectation for inquiry, critical thinking, and self-structured learning. Outcomes in those areas can be fostered and assessed in the normal course of student progression toward a degree or certificate. Thus, one could evaluate student achievement of lifelong learning by evaluating the student's application of these skills and abilities in an informal, self-initiated, self-structured environment.

Since technology is increasingly an enabling tool for lifelong learning, institutions can prepare students for the use of technology in a learning context by requiring them to demonstrate basic learning-related technology skills. These skills can be acquired in a stand-alone course, such as an online-only class, that is entirely dependent on technology. They can also be acquired through a hybrid – traditionally delivered and technology-delivered – course that requires the use of technology as part of the learning process. To foster development of critical thinking, students can be required to demonstrate basic information-literacy skills, which can be acquired in a stand-alone course or acquired as a required element of a discipline-based course. To demonstrate effectiveness of informal, self-directed learning, students can be required to identify learning objectives, specify indicators of success in achieving the objectives, develop a strategy for achieving the objectives, and demonstrate, assess, and document achievement of the learning objectives. These abilities can be acquired through a project-based learning activity, either as a stand-alone independent learning class or as a component of a required capstone class.

Table 2. Implementation Considerations

SUGGESTIONS FOR EFFECTIVE PRACTICE
1. Develop a glossary to foster a common understanding of terms.
2. Identify intended outcomes and indicators of achievement.
3. Identify the purpose for assessment.
4. Establish a review of outcomes assessment as part of curriculum review.
5. Create an inventory of assessment strategies, methods, and tools.
6. Collect, analyze, and evaluate data consistent with the intended outcome.
7. Ensure assessment results are integrated in a natural manner with planning to improve practice.
8. Establish the relevance of assessment to personal, program, and institutional practice.

A Lesson From Stone

A number of emerging trends will significantly affect the future for community and technical colleges. Chief among them is a rise in the importance of credentialing student achievements (Gardiner, 1994). In the future, an even greater premium will be placed on explicit evidence, rather than inferences, of achievements. Thus, assessment and documentation of student knowledge, skills, abilities, and attitudes will be elevated to a higher level of awareness and action. As assessing and certifying student achievements become paramount within the academy, instruction will shift from a primary function to a support function as a means for students to achieve desired outcomes.

In making this transition, it is critical that actions and assessments align with achievements in the natural rhythm of institutional life. A study of the manner by which stone masons integrate design, construction, and quality control in daily activities may aid in understanding how academic masons can integrate planning, actions, and assessments as normal practice within the academic community.

When approaching a project, a stone mason considers a number of factors: (1) the object to be built; (2) artistic, financial, and structural constraints; (3) necessary preparatory work; (4) sequence and timeline for actions; (5) materials that should be used; and (6) maintenance of quality control during construction. In short, the mason must align and integrate intentions, actions, and assessments integrated with planning and construction.

For the sake of this metaphor, assume the mason is to build a functional but decorative retaining wall. In preparing a design, the mason must consider both artistic and engineering implications. Upon completion of the design, attention turns to selection of appropriate construction materials and methods, including preparation of the foundation necessary to support the wall. To aid in keeping the wall straight during construction, a tightly drawn string is used to align the connecting sections with the beginning and ending points of the wall. Mortar is used to anchor the stones or bricks, but before it is allowed to dry, the mason checks to make sure the wall remains plumb and straight as construction proceeds.

Thus, a stone mason fulfills multiple tasks in the normal course of daily events. Intended outcomes and constraints are translated into an appropriate design, requisite materials are selected and gathered, an appropriate foundation is prepared consistent with the function of the final product, and the wall is constructed in an environment of simultaneous and continuous assessment of progress to ensure the principles of the project are preserved and intended outcomes are realized.

In the same manner, members of the academic community must integrate assessment into educational practice as a naturally occurring event to demonstrate congruence of intentions, actions, and achievements. In addition to enhancing quality and effectiveness, aligning institutional practices provides a contextually rich framework of incremental steps leading from intentions to acquisition to assessment and documentation and finally to improvements for the future. (See Figure 4.)

A model of educational practice based upon definition of intentions, alignment of actions, assessment of achievements, and evidence of outcomes fosters internal consistency with institutional values and provides a framework to inform student progress, document institutional integrity and effectiveness, and evaluate student achievements. Nonetheless, development and application of meaningful, authentic assessment of achievements of both social-based and economic-based outcomes is a formidable challenge (Alfred, Ewell, Hudgins, & McClenny, 1999). Community and technical colleges *can* overcome the challenge and *will* overcome the challenge, because they *must* overcome the challenge if traditional community college values and outcomes are to persist.

Figure 4. Alignment and Congruence of Intentions, Actions, and Achievements

The primary purpose of this monograph is to provoke thought and promote dialogue on educational quality and effectiveness in achieving intended outcomes. To fulfill that purpose, an operational framework is developed to aid in analysis of key educational practices and synthesis of relationship among those practices. That framework serves as a guide to align intentions, actions, and achievements. Table 3 represents that framework as a series of reflective questions.

More than a basis for philosophical discussions, the framework and related questions form a foundation for workshop activities that result in institutional actions. For example, following confirmation of institutional values and intentions as reflected in the mission statement, list what the institution actually does – its actions. If they can not be listed under one or more institutional outcome, perhaps they are isolated anecdotal activities that are not part of the institution's mission. Alternatively, it could mean they are important and the institution's mission should be expanded to include what the institution is actually doing. Repeat the exercise for institutional unit and academic program intentions.

Table 3. Implementation Considerations

FRAMING QUESTIONS TO GUIDE EFFECTIVE PRACTICE	
Principles and Values	Who are we?
Mission and Purpose	What will we do?
Vision	Where are we going?
Intended Outcomes	What do we expect to achieve?
Planning and Goals	How will we proceed?
Actions	What steps are we taking to realize our intentions?
Quality and Effectiveness	Do we achieve our intended outcomes and fulfill our intentions?
Assessment	How do we know?
Evidence	What do we have to substantiate achievements and outcomes?
Assimilation	What are we doing with the results of our assessments?

Epilogue

Achieving the purpose of a professional publication is frequently assumed by virtue of its publication. However, reliance on implications and inferences of achievement is contrary to the spirit of effective practice outlined in this monograph. The framework in Table 4 is constructed to adhere to the principles of context and alignment by applying those principles in a natural coherent fashion to the monograph itself.

There is ample opportunity for disagreement on the content of this framework, especially with regard to assessing achievement of purpose. The point of this activity is not to debate the individual choice of indicators of success, actions taken to achieve the intended outcome, strategy for data collection, method of analysis, basis for evaluation, form of evidence, or use of assessment findings. The point is to demonstrate that these elements can be considered individually and aligned collectively in a reasonable manner to evaluate whether the intended outcome is achieved while simultaneously informing personal and professional directions for future practice.

Table 4. Alignment of Intentions, Actions, and Achievements

MONOGRAPH ASSESSMENT	
Intention	Provoke thought and promote dialogue on effective educational practice
Success Indicator	Publication by professional organization; minimum of 50 survey* responses with at least 75% agreement or disagreement with author's perspective
Actions	State perspectives, reinforce with examples, pose reflective questions
Data Collection*	Self-assessment, reader survey, informal feedback
Data Analysis	Analyze distribution of responses to objective questions; analyze feedback and responses to open-ended questions to identify themes and patterns
Evaluation	Identify areas of success (see above); draw conclusions regarding the merit and relevance of the topics in provoking thought on effective practice
Evidence	Published monograph; summary of survey responses, including comments
Assimilation	Findings used to determine relevance, merit, and subsequent activities

*Readers are invited and encouraged to complete the online survey at www.league.org/survey/aic.

References

Ackoff, R. L. (1995). *From Mechanistic to Social Systemic Thinking* [Videotape]. (Tape number V9303). Cambridge, MA: Pegasus Communications, Inc.

Alfred, R., Ewell, P., Hudgins, J., & McClenney, K. (1999). *Core Indicators of Effectiveness for Community Colleges.* Washington, DC: Community College Press.

An Assessment Framework for Community Colleges. (2004). Questionmark Corporation and League for Innovation in the Community College. Available at www.league.org/publication/whitepapers/0804.html.

Angelo, T. A. (2002). Engaging and Supporting Faculty in the Scholarship of Assessment: Guidelines from Research and Practice. In T. W. Banta (Ed.), *Building a Scholarship of Assessment* (pp. 185-200). San Francisco: Jossey-Bass.

Baker, R. L. (2001). Educational Cartography: Mapping the Learning Outcomes Frontier. *Michigan Community College Journal, 7*(1), 79-87. (ERIC Document Reproduction Service No. ED 628 411).

Baker, R. L. (2004). Keystones of Regional Accreditation: Intentions, Outcomes, and Sustainability. In P. Hernon (Ed.), *Outcomes Assessment in Higher Education: Views and Perspectives* (pp. 1-15). Westport, CT: Libraries Unlimited.

Banta, T. W. (2002). Characteristics of Effective Outcomes Assessment: Foundations and Examples. In T. W. Banta (Ed.), *Building a Scholarship of Assessment* (pp. 261-283). San Francisco: Jossey-Bass.

Boggs, G. R. (1995). The Paradigm for Community Colleges – Who's Leading the Way? *Catalyst, 25*(1), 27-28.

Carver, J. (1997). *Boards that Make a Difference* (2nd ed.). San Francisco: Jossey-Bass.

Community College Survey of Student Engagement. (2004). *Engagement by Design*. Austin, TX: Author.

Ewell, P. T. (1994). A Matter of Integrity: Accountability and the Future of Self-Regulation. *Change, 26*(6), 24-29.

Ewell, P. T. (2002). An Emerging Scholarship: A Brief History of Assessment. In T. W. Banta (Ed.), *Building a Scholarship of Assessment* (pp. 3-25). San Francisco: Jossey-Bass.

Gardiner, L. F. (1994). *Redesigning Higher Education: Producing Dramatic Gains in Student Learning*. ASHE-ERIC Higher Education Report, *23*(7). Washington, DC: The George Washington University, Graduate School of Education and Human Development.

Gray, P. T. (2002). The Roots of Assessment: Tensions, Solutions, and Research Directions. In T. W. Banta (Ed.), *Building a Scholarship of Assessment* (pp. 49-66). San Francisco: Jossey-Bass.

Kelly, M. (1993). Taming the Demons of Change. *Business Ethics, 7*(4), 6-7.

Munitz, B. (1995). Wanted: New Leadership for Higher Education. *Planning for Higher Education, 24*(1), 9-16.

O'Bannion, T. (1997). *Creating More Learning-Centered Community Colleges*. Mission Viejo, CA: League for Innovation in the Community College.

Pike, G. R. (2002). Measurement Issues in Outcomes Assessment. In T. W. Banta (Ed.), *Building a Scholarship of Assessment* (pp. 131-147). San Francisco: Jossey-Bass.

Peters, R. (1994). Some Snarks are Boojums: Accountability and the End(s) of Higher Education. *Change, 26*(6), 16-23.

Wilson, C. D., Miles, C. L., Baker. R. L., & Schoenberger, R. L. (2000). *Learning Outcomes for the 21st Century: Report of a Community College Study*. Mission Viejo, CA: League for Innovation in the Community College. (ERIC Document Reproduction Service No. ED 439 751).

Wolff, R. A. and Harris, O. D. (1994). Using Assessment to Develop a Culture of Evidence. In D. G. Halpem, (Ed.), *Changing College Classrooms: New Teaching and Learning Strategies for an Increasingly Complex World* (pp. 271-288). San Francisco: Jossey-Bass. (ERIC Document Reproduction Service No. ED 368 307).

About the Author

Ronald L. Baker is the Deputy Executive Director of the Northwest Commission on Colleges and Universities.* Prior to joining the commission, he was the chief academic officer at Cascadia Community College where he directed the development of its outcomes-based curriculum. He was also a national facilitator for the 21st Century Learning Outcomes Project and a consultant for the Learning College Project, both led by the League for Innovation in the Community College. His experience in higher education includes service at the state level as the Director of Distance Education for the Oregon community colleges as well as service at the campus as a director of academic technology, division chair, and 14 years as a full-time community college faculty member.

Ron has given numerous presentations and written several articles on distance education, learning outcomes, and outcomes assessment. He holds a B.A. in Mathematics from Washington State University, an M.S. in Mathematics from New Mexico State University, an M.S. in Computer Education from Eastern Washington University, and an Ed.D. in Community College Leadership from Oregon State University.

*The views expressed in this monograph are those of the author and should not be attributed to the board, staff, or member institutions of the Northwest Commission on Colleges and Universities.